equilibrium's form

Also by Susanne Dyckman:

Counterweight (Woodland Editions chapbook)

Transiting Indigo (EtherDome Press chapbook)

equilibrium's form

Susanne Dyckman

Shearsman Books
Exeter

First published in the United Kingdom in 2007 by
Shearsman Books Ltd
58 Velwell Road
Exeter EX4 4LD   www.shearsman.com

ISBN-13 978-1-905700-20-2   ISBN-10 1-905700-20-2

Acknowledgements

Grateful acknowledgement is given to the following journals in which
some of these poems have appeared, often in earlier versions and with
different titles: *Pomona Valley Review, Five Fingers Review, Switchback* and
Marginalia.

In the poem 'following her geometry', the italicized line, '*a small thing fits
into a small hand*', is from Elizabeth Robinson's poem 'Treasure Chest'.
Also, the poems titled 'apparent horizon', 'from a distance', 'convocation',
and 'forgetting was only temporary' draw on the writings of Kabir and
Antonin Artaud.

Four of these poems were included in the chapbook *Counterweight*
(Woodland Editions), and sections of this book were first published
as the chapbook *Transiting Indigo* (EtherDome). I wish to express my
appreciation to the editors, Jaime Robles (Woodland Editions), and
Colleen Lookingbill and Elizabeth Robinson (EtherDome).

I give thanks to, and for, my son, Ryan Bennett, and to my family and
friends, always. I am deeply grateful to Tony Frazer for his support and
patience. Patricia Dienstfrey, Todd Melicker, Jaime Robles and Brian Teare
graciously read and commented on the work. A special blessing is given
to Elizabeth Robinson for her insight, encouragement, and milagros.

The publisher gratefully acknowledges financial assistance from
Arts Council England.

contents

For my sister,
Christina Marie Preddy

how a life is made

sky bone arm

eye

what is known is

dusk silence hand scar

not a sound but

word

air

storm   syllable   the more precise

wave   determined and to

white

damp of clinging   star   thought   skin   fire

history

I live in an arid climate, but what I know is rain. Puddles that form in the lows of the yard, the dampness of the walls. The skylight dripping onto the kitchen table, so I have to hold the morning paper aside to keep it from getting wet. Water pools on the threshold and I roll up an old towel to block it. There is rot on the windowsills, spots where I can poke my finger into the wood. Spiders build nests under the eaves of the roof. Fog rolls over the house morning and afternoon. The paint on the siding peels, a wall of open lips.

sitting with words

i.

a torn vestment

a color of night   the more precise

vista of melting ice

that is   an inebriating weave

rippled as early glass

or the lift of the horizon

sliding over embankments

or the left unsaid

being broken water

ii.

dipping fingers

in shadow play

is all I know

unplumbed   quaking

every word sought is

collected and distilled

wormwood and a winding sheet

lead never gold

— I am your sleeping —

water: collection

as my legs grow numb

and the fingers of my hand that collect shells

turn numb

I fix to the tide-

waters'

rustling

                a bit of wood and bone reveal

all that was   all that asked

postscript

& gone   but warned the day before   *goodbye was too hard*

& what to do with bottled vetiver   why she likes it so

(more at jonquil   more at diminished)

in saying   *determined* to take a warmer region

collecting and to put   would she?   breathe   not hold

to drive down that street, which is the way I usually go . . .

of course   &

                    — in a lengthy tête-à-tête

how to say   of where we are   conversation is not a quest

absurdly   *it didn't work*

from any locale someone leaves the will to be

every step & after

now gone   sense of static, turning to the radio

soundings

or   as cowed   frightened into

submission

compliant cycling arms

advice   never depend on others

— omitted —

admit

empty oyster   lackluster   points of meringue

      damp of pearly fog

      to kiss   as low to ground

        as is

              base

      looking for stops

inside

                to interrupt

from any chosen point

foot   cold pacing
             a matter of

         tile under

the honed

flint   retracting   heals

syllables hidden   behind

more syllables   there's the scar

short   where the long and lovely word

                              lingers

                                        a back arched in sand

        the surface   elbows   feet   sprawl

or

        bird song returns song

     others counter / to mirror

that curiosity / flying bones

history

The ocean is on our right as we start down the mile-long stretch of white sand, arm in arm. There is a dampness around her mouth, even though the wind is blowing and my lips are starting to crack in the sunlight. She smiles with her moist mouth and hands me her canned drink to hold while she tightens the white scarf knotted under her chin. We are almost the same height and weight, like twins, except her walk is slow and I need to hold back to match her pace. Her skin is brown, not a healthy brown but a shade of sickness. She's cold so I take my blue quilted jacket and give it to her to wear. She gives me, in exchange, her black and orange shawl. It makes my skin itch.

home

everything must be arranged   the table   its marred wood

the back door as it slams

        stay where you are

             the space of possibility

   is an appetite   a piece of newsprint as it blows away

   the shadow
      no one
       can influence

  bending light in a tiger's eye

    stay   be still   you are stone

urgency of the canyon

light is not haunting but ubiquitous

when you look at the sky

that is death

places of darkness turned

shimmering and luminescent

I begin the plea

to the good gutter   maybe there

the broken string of an impossible word

maybe there the glass Venetian rosary

to grind in my palms

everything illuminates

even fires

burnt out and sucked back

into the vortex of lightlessness

from the bottom

of the canyon

I track your

lucent body

a figure

of five points

yet with all the graces

essential to

white-winged rendering   your leap across

entry 10.06

moving through me
                              trying to enclose
                tomorrow

a great bird come to pass over

I will the shadow
swallowing whole

tenancy

walking through your fenceless
        land   I would watch your left

hand break the silence   as a marble slab
eager to be split   then sculpted into other

form   I would
be you   would give

all a breeze wants
      a wave building up before my eyes

the sweeping away of old shavings
      at last   confetti at your feet   plum blossoms

obligation of service

were voice scent

memory in a molting peach sky

would spark one thousand permutations

as it rains again

more than I can hold

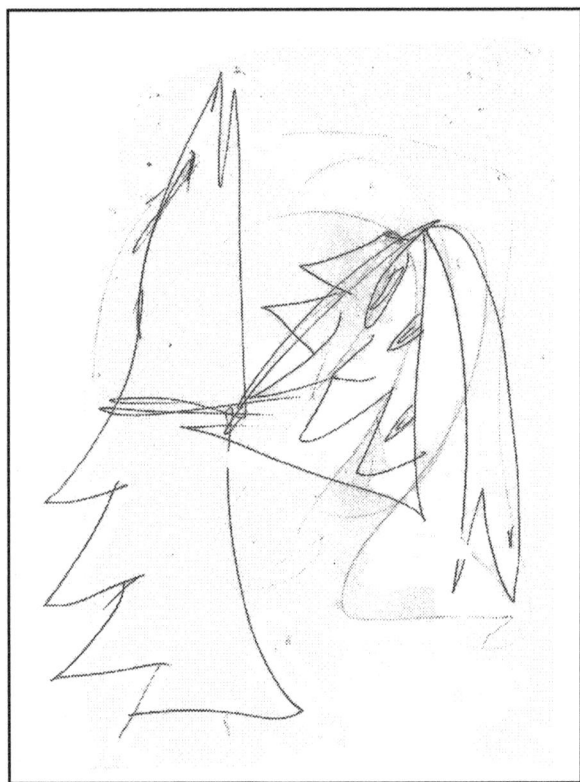

entry 05.25

fingers find the shirt
open   find another
shirt beneath   unbutton that
and still no skin

invocation

pale panoramas   something to remake

    is spirit no longer anything?

        to dust this instrument of dust returns

    this body   I will do it again and again

    lead the world to zero   evoke melodies

apparent horizon

that swing never ceases its sway in the middle of the road

streams of light flow to the one delay in all directions concrete

unidentified debris lost in contemplation not a sound

to be plucked from this place where unstruck music sounds of itself

or the driver seems to have no head or behind the wheel is the sky

thinking of a scene: a shoe   the sinkhole under

the chassis a story that holds true for some and for some never

crossing to the scent of sandal and flowers cleared away

history

Her eyes are changing. The deep brown of her iris is spreading out into the surrounding white. There are no distinct borders anymore, no black edges to mark where the color stops. The center breaks apart, fragments floating like small islands in the sea of her eye. No one warned. My mouth makes a little gasping noise and my shoulders tighten. What's happening to her eyes? The sky outside the windows is pitch-black. There's no rising moon, no sun, just the in-between.

notes for the 9th month

quail worry at smoke and distance

     fire is turning hills   brittle

   her bed is perched

      not far from the break

               beyond the door

      the dust blows pink

heat rises because it does

her last breath

rises because

the week of cycling flame

attends   waiting to be filled

to be fed   fulfillment

enough

days of the month

the greatest danger

is not flame but final

words slurred

or written as a note

the sun blinds my left eye

a cotton apron

in yellow flower print

two pockets   sash tie

what remains

coincidence of crackling air

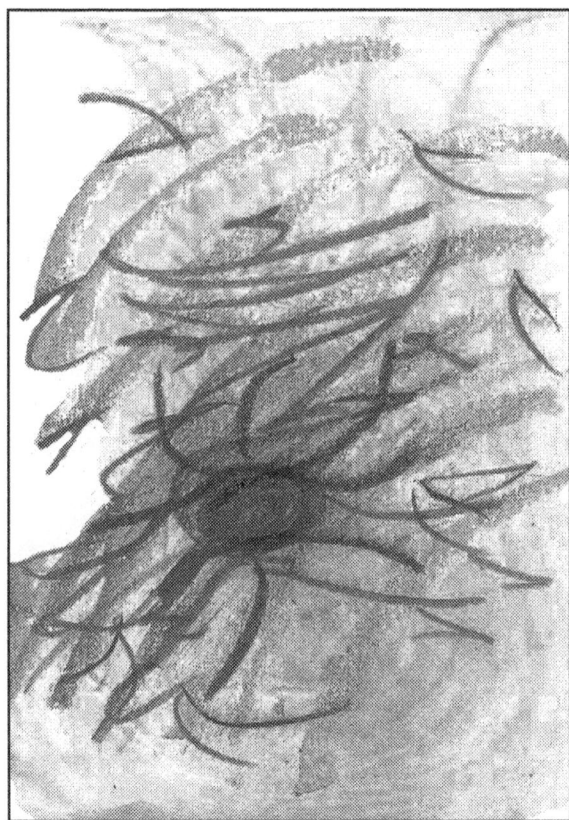

for want

I am searching the oceans to inform

waves   tidal foam

not a spirit made   contented

but interferences enjoyed:

                salt in the mouth

           action taking place in no visible scene

heritage

first the ceremony of sword & knife

                                 (to remove the past)

then the flecks at dawn

                                 (insert hope)

                 minutia

                 slices

                 the

                 air

                 lands as rubble

                          landing as gauze

(a coin falls in the well)

category four

i.

my hand in twilight
half opens   (the portal

exposing crimson
on bone)   a death's-head painted

against orange fingers it hovers
in cavernous space   the small body leans

— like draws like — against me   moth
wing staining skin indigo

ii.

a day is itself only at the end   twilight

catches the in-between   a portal

blurs as time loses its crimson

edge   what's done is   the poppy painted

too bright   (insipid in a vase)   to hover

over this thought or to be erased one leans

into shade   drawn moth-

like   to the sky   transiting indigo

entry 00.00

before you trying not to look purple but looking purple
the inner corner of the lid eases into a crescent blending
into the fleshy cheek eyes so much less than
the sockets carved in the face
a nervous habit
a hand-me-down fit: sleeves drooping beyond fingers
shoulders hit elbows
one button brushes the top of the knee
an old bruise rises

history

The hallway is long and immaculate and empty. I'm on the fourth floor, the sun is bright through the western window. I've claimed a chair, one with wooden arms, upholstered in brown and purple fabric. The cushions have been protected with a glossy silicone spray, so the backs and thighs of a hundred restless people, sitting, then standing, then sitting again, rubbing their clothing and coats against the fabric, will never leave a mark. The doctor walks past me in his green surgical scrubs. His posture is perfect, his body gives off no warmth. I'm startled by his fingers, long and slender, like a concert pianist's. I scurry to catch him.

equilibrium's form

in the story on the path (ribbon of dirt)

nerves meet glass

a fall is (felt)

the wound is (felt)

here a different flesh takes hold   mid-forehead's

dagger

on skin

a hallowed

surprise

our shared aspirate

unspeakable but called residue

the mind in its cradle

the mind humming to itself

the self gauging its size by movement

given a name that cannot be spelled

timorous

with discontent

the fore and hind

having trouble   relating

to abundance   to water   conveyed to   the body

(sound of night fire)

not holding the sky

not searching

(but illumed

by rifle shot)

a blue that was meant to be

brown

kaleidoscoping light

a composition unfolded

in equal percentages

for the skull's

suspect parts

solutions   poured in then spit

from the mouth   rattling small doses

now distinct

        yet again   not thinking

    who or where known by the finger's trace

                    across the scar turned pink

vellum held to the skin turning pink

what to leave

an island paradise off course

a lemon or a willow branch battered by the wind

all tangible proof   certain as the fabric spun by worms

slowly

leave this behind

forgiveness for the dead

who are growing repetitious

the untenable freedom of birds

a testament of thieves

water: turning

a stalk of love-lies-bleeding

is in typical collapse

intermittent

the bloom

(I am here and now I am

        here   but less so)

is a witnessed event   red-green as the

sea and as jealous   it stokes its own movement

in a dream of dancing shoes —

black flats   elastic over the arch

entry 06.03

              the gods
sweep down from god heights to choose the world
         a gigolo a cheat
the herald the waving tongue
         the hustler turned Gabriel turned mockingbird
a kite in the air flushing clouds   a kitchen knife I stand against
the lost of a last breed

water: calling

vulnerable   one sinks

                (surface tension transports)

under the wonder of a wash

       (nothing will turn it

                    away) this need

is – true or false –   like symbols, changeable

                 and also soft

and breathless   even

          with resistance

             a force

that repeats   (unconquered   unscathed   absorbed)

    all manner of
    calling me to the edge, beckoning

entry 01.06

gold to conduct the sun

tourmaline to keep away

myrrh to anoint at birth and death

copal for making sacred

history

Pain is visible on his face, a kind of scarring. It's a tense look, something in the way the skin holds to the bones and around the eyes. I won't ever be able to see him again as completely relaxed, and even when he'll appear to be at ease, I'll know. His fingers will unconsciously push against his forehead and his focus will shift. He'll be in battle, the pressure in his head an impenetrable barrier between how he feels and what he wants.

entry 10.29

I stare at this map and I do not know it as myself

.

following her geometry

i.

as patterns come undone

       everyone is closing in to see

how stone rotates in circles   how twelve can become six

or six become the sole taker

a snake repeats circumference

ii.

restore the old measurements

a small thing fits into a small hand

inches and inch-worms triangulate

a series of actions

where a tree makes the perfect arc

iii.

at twice the pace   absence is crossed out

sections drawn

            on one side or the other

become equivalents

                            angles too close to angels

            a set of pointing moons

entry 10.17 (1)

perpetually unshod I am taken to the river
here the blessing of water lasts
while fumes from burning
towers dissipate with time

I ask to be taught
with fire

to learn the way of difficult breath

winter apart

so huddled in the cold

I could be a knot   the alley's paper

scraps curl up   in flames

someone pens across the skin   exposed between my coat

and glove   *forgive*

though the wind should fold and leave   an ash floats in

above my head

impertinent   a third-eye's violence

or protective sign much like

the star that speeds its course   while dying   to the sun

on the edges of the sky   there could be fires

or be Venus   or the holy oil

to be used for benediction   at once   the city's milky

doors all close   in darkening

the measure of your length

recalled   if it were   your hand conspiring with mine

from a distance

        an instant of intelligence

           plunging into the field of night

becomes

      empty and

wandering

        I have lost all as I slept

entry 08.18

it is as if one giant fly were hovering over   sucking air
with his thousand eyes   and beneath him
my over-shadowed face   forgetting his very deafness
that his hunger gnaws like mine

cloud

memorize this assemblage —

cracked stone   the flume of sky

to grow apprehensive as vapor collects

is less an act than a picturing

engulfed   the day begins descent as it arrives

mist veers from its trail   those

left behind are called grounded

may be called gatherers   wool   spun-sugar

or dangled from a pocket stitched to hide

one inch of thread

entry 08.09

red built burned raised again the color of drying blood the color
of the floor in a flat alarming & almost orange already weathered
at birth out of the can a color that can't decide its lacquer red luck
prayers or a message of silk telegrams
squared enamel strokes   heavenly   a brush with

convocation

when the wave rises

when the wave washes

over   it is water   when it falls it is water falling

(it is the water   again falling over the naming)

because it has been named   the naming taken as wave

the name no longer is

marginalia

drifting

street- wise

                      (gangly body
visioned larger than   color through fingers
                streamlets in muddied air)

something not detailed but here:

likeness of damp objects at dusk

water: watching

after I say she was taken
        I mean by the waters
        I mean by droplets

               on the floor

she is certain to survive
her drink of the sea   upwelling   where a cure from
               is a pinch   spoonful   dash
               silica ash

kin to crystalline sweetness

        the grit left on flesh needed

        as when I say it was a silver element

            I mean it was soundless

entry 10.17 (2)

to remember: to re-member
to put yourself together again

forgetting was only temporary

these worlds   these unnumbered objects

where the way is made

are purely and simply

synaptic overspill

gestures of Krishnas with folded hands

Indras who dwell   in the sky   as stains

every two weeks

when the collapse
of all the words
arrives
and pyramids of thought
drift in a gritty storm
the past might pivot
dialects never learned
returning as a new
layer of skin

       where will it end   a dress

dropping spangles
the body as it moves in sequences of rain

shape of morning

lush as moss

we whisper in a different tongue

                yours or mine

grasses tearing apart

cradling

hands cupped   ( )

closed   your eyes   let hands

(   )   hands

      let them
lace fingers   be   let them
    fall   cup   hands

   closed

     eyes

       (   )   let

hands

          let

    fall

        fingers   eyes

         laced

Born in Chicago, Susanne Dyckman has lived on both coasts of the U.S., finally settling in Albany, California, where she curates the Evelyn Avenue reading series. She is the author of two chapbooks, and is on the editorial staff of *Five Fingers Review*. She is currently a thesis advisor for the University of San Francisco's MFA in Writing program.